Get Fit

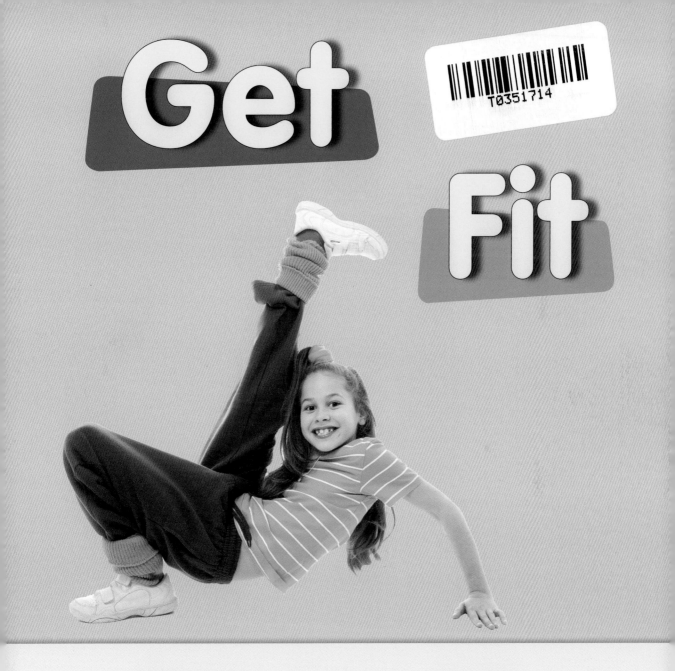

Written by Lucy Smith

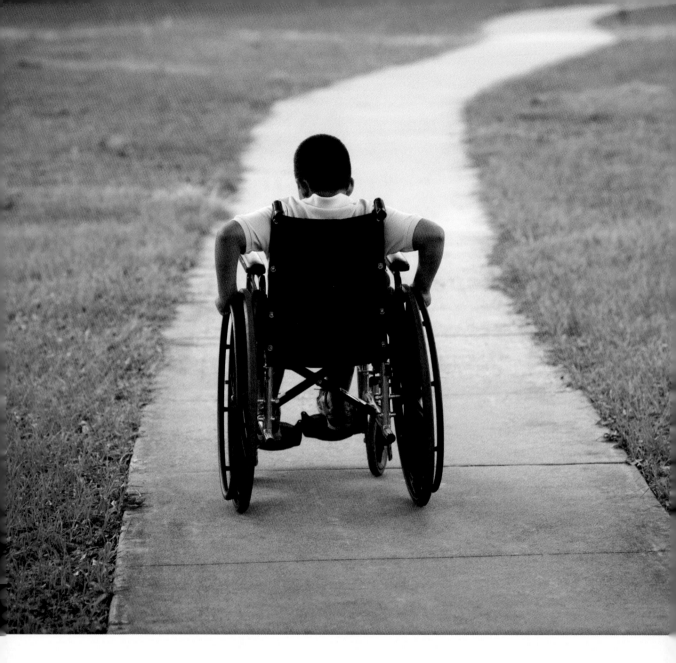

I go up the hill.

2

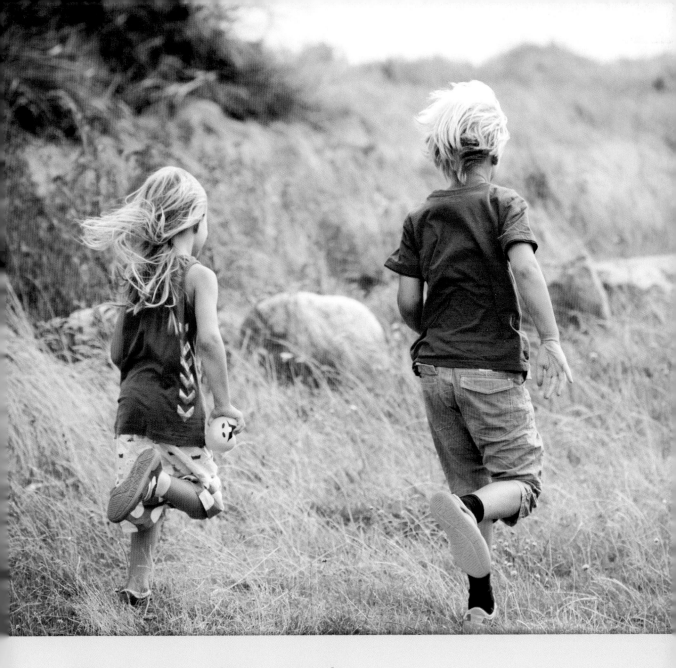

Run to the rock.

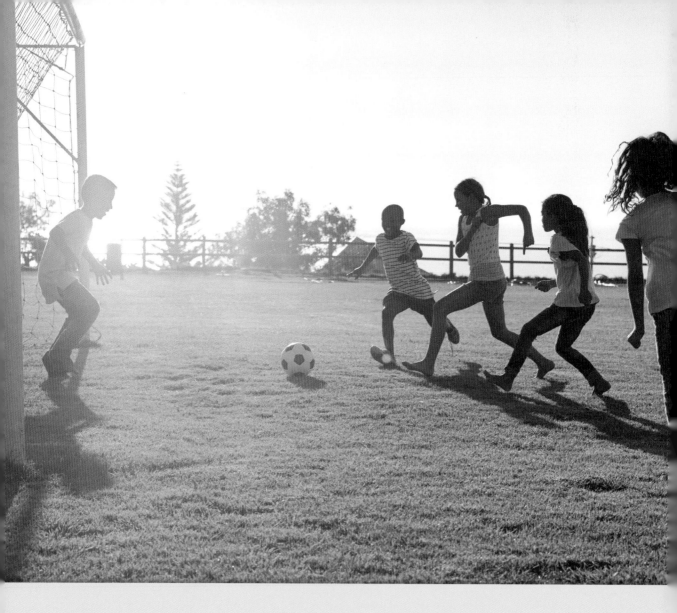

Pass it!
I can kick it into the net.

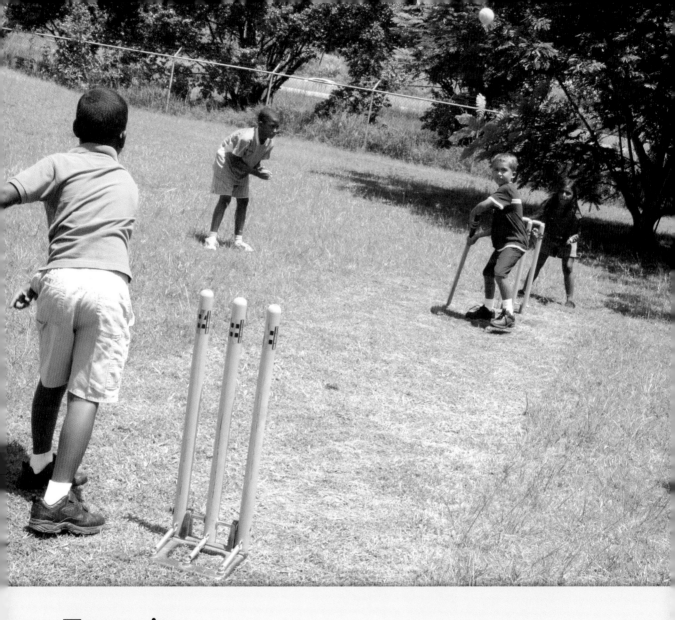

Toss it.
Can I hit it?

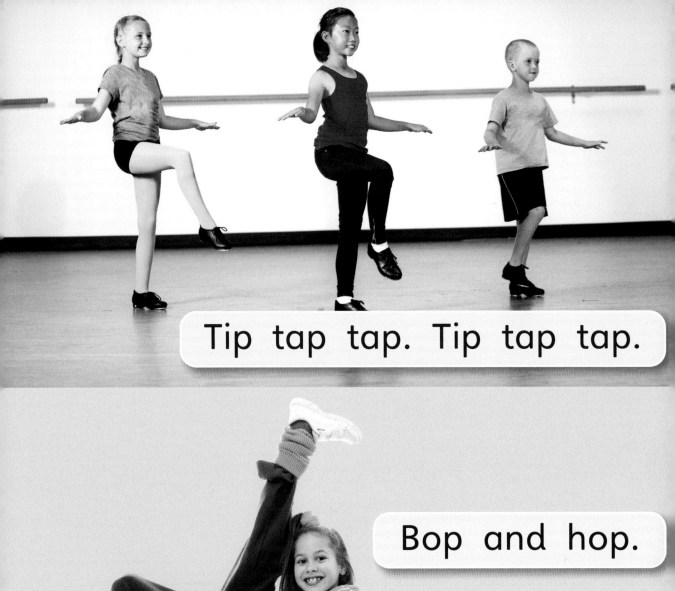

Tip tap tap. Tip tap tap.

Bop and hop.

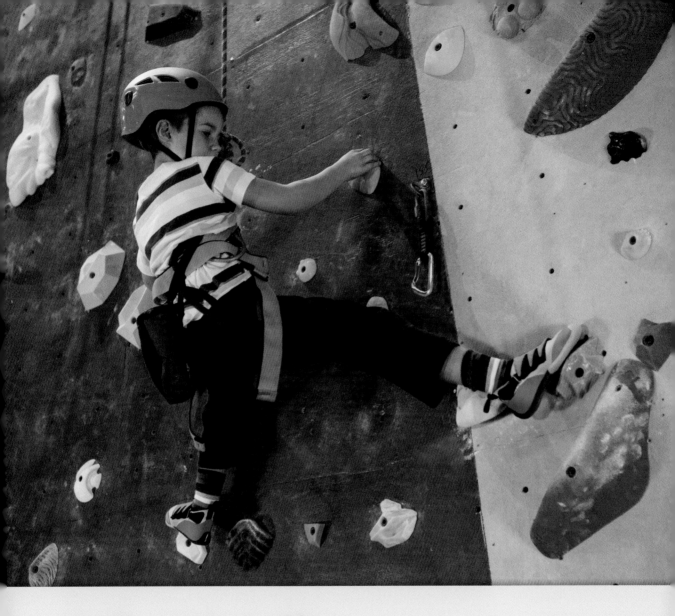

Huff and puff!
I can get up to the top.

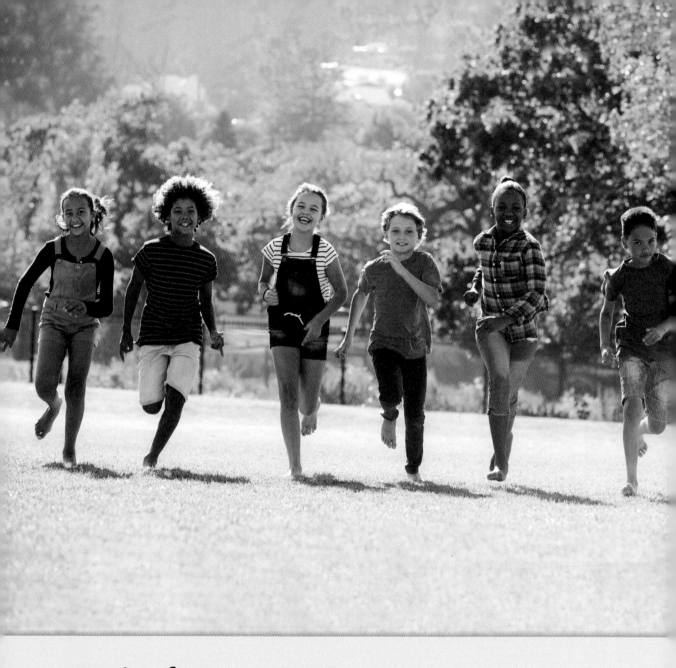

It is fun!